Christmas Joy

ISBN 0-7935-4702-4

7777 W. Bluemound Rd. P.O. Box 13819 Milwaukee, WI 53213

Deck The Hall

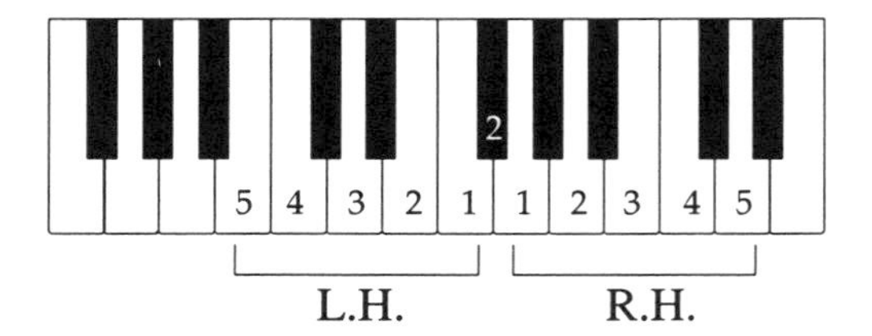

Traditional

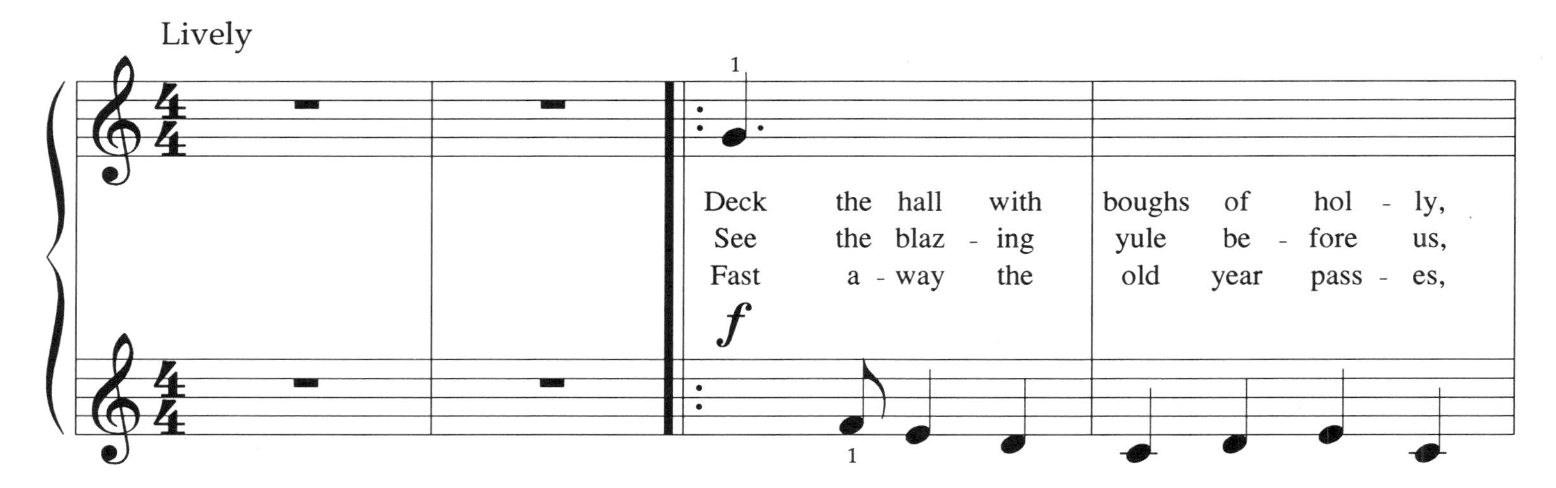

Duet Part (Student plays one octave higher.)

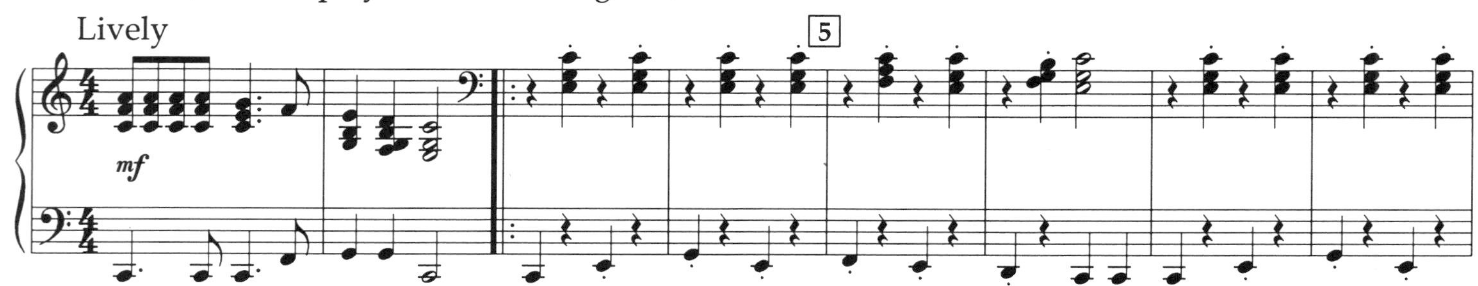

9
1
fa la la la la, la la la la. Don we now our gay ap-par - el,
fa la la la la, la la la la. Fol - low me in mer - ry meas-ure,
fa la la la la, la la la la. Sing we joy - ous, all to-geth - er,
13
2 1
fa la la la la la la la la. Troll the an - cient
fa la la la la la la la la. While I tell of
fa la la la la la la la la. Heed - less of the
16
1.,2.
3.
yule - tide car - ol, fa la la la la, la la la la.
yule - tide treas - ure, fa la la la la, la la la la.
wind and weath - er, fa la la la la, la la la la.
9
13
16
1.,2.
3.

Go Tell It On The Mountain

Traditional

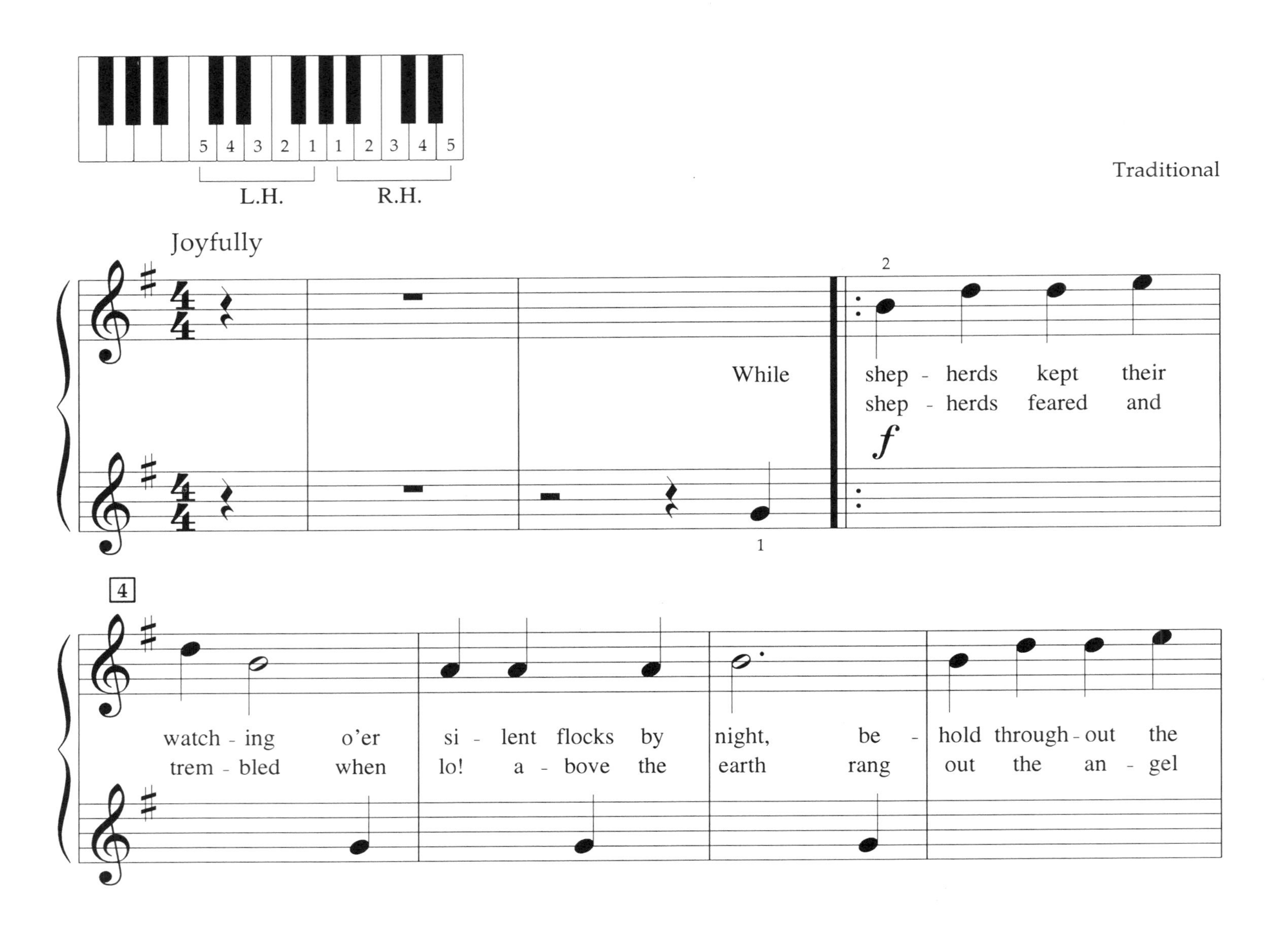

Duet Part (Student plays one octave higher.)

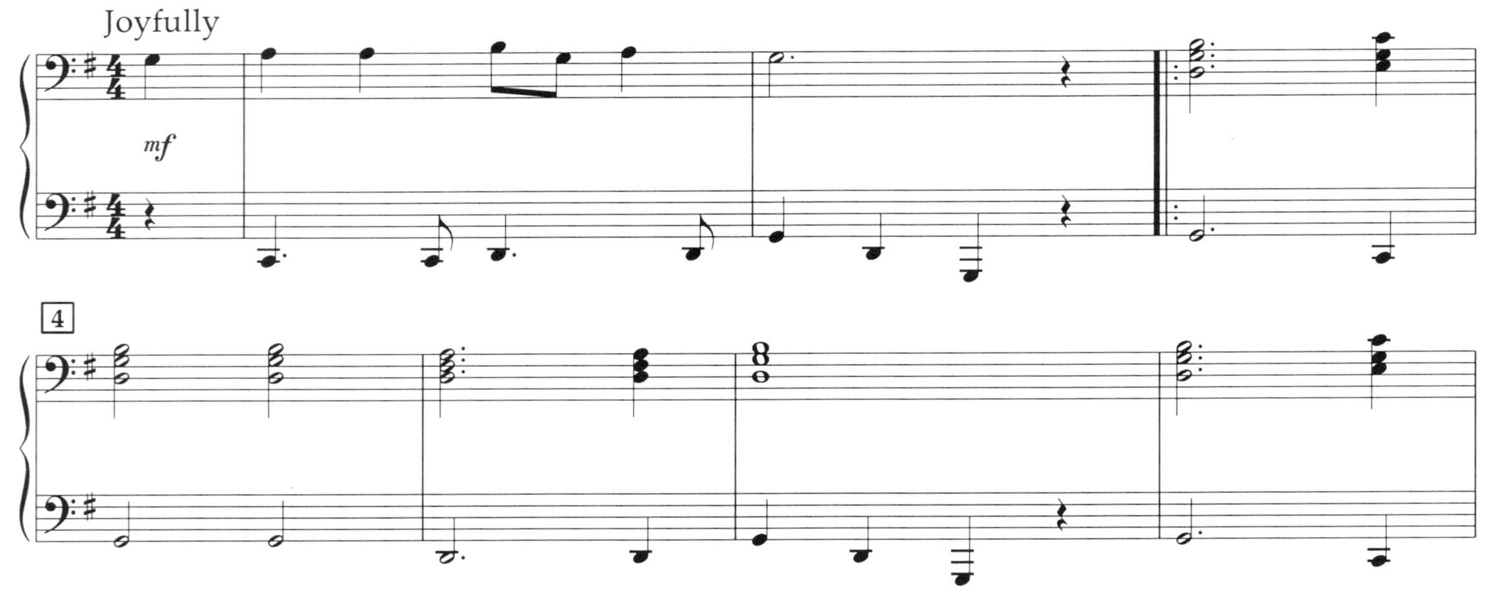

8
heav - ens there shone a ho - ly light.
cho - rus that hailed our Sav - ior's birth.
Go, tell it on the
12
moun - tain o - ver the hills and ev - ery - where, go, tell it on the
16
moun - tain that Je - sus Christ is born. The born.
1.
2.
8
12
16
1.
2.

Good King Wenceslas

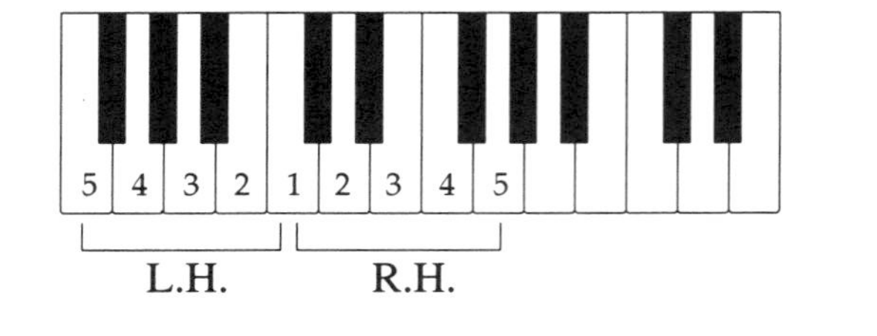

Traditional

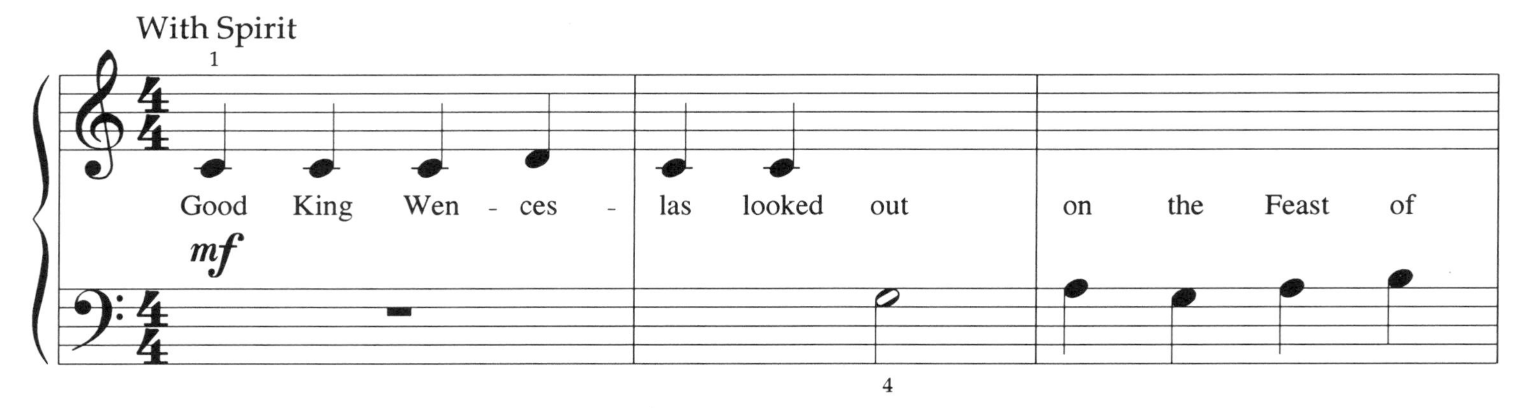

Duet Part (Student plays one octave higher.)

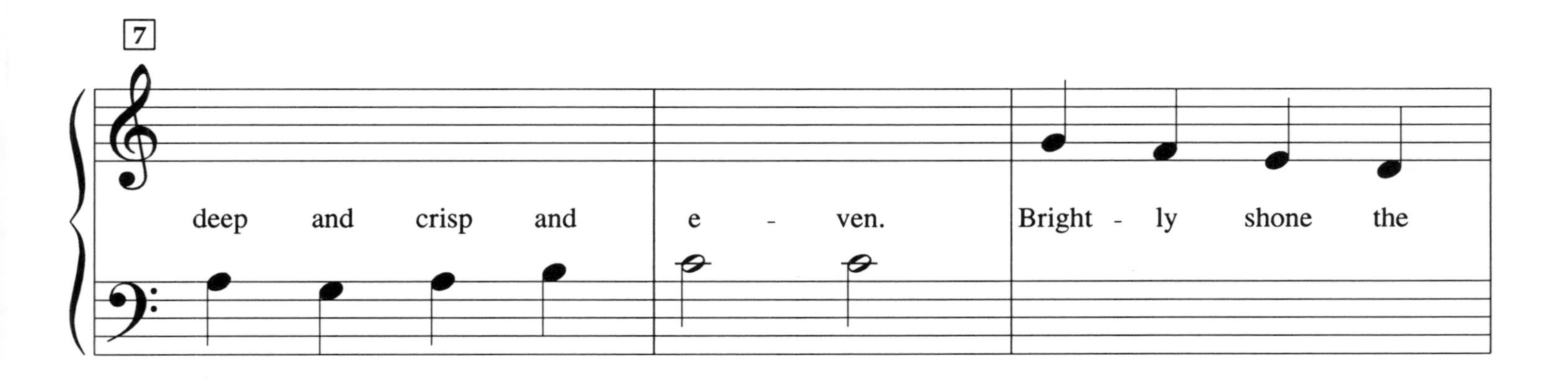
7
deep and crisp and e - ven. Bright - ly shone the

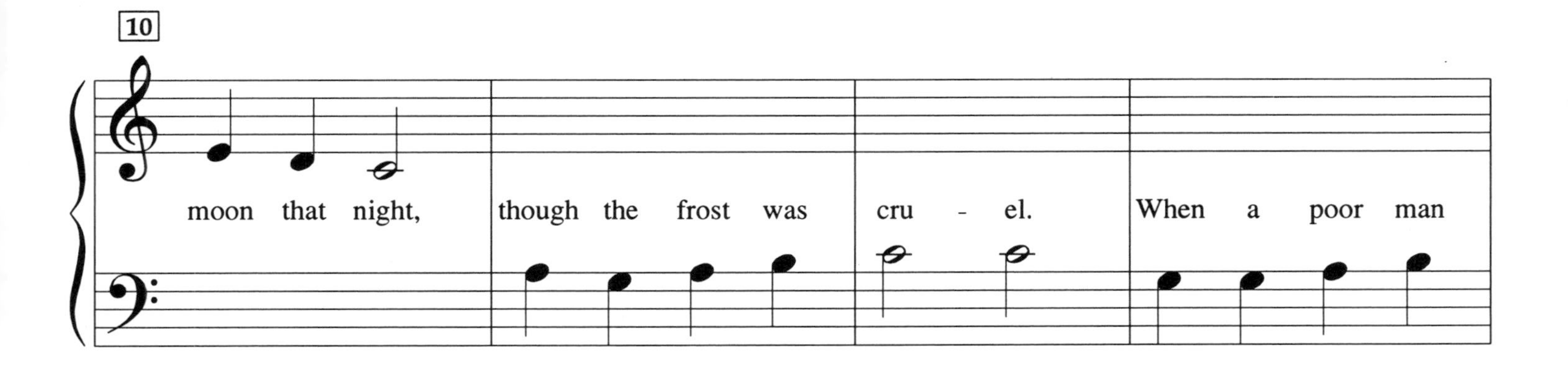
10
moon that night, though the frost was cru - el. When a poor man

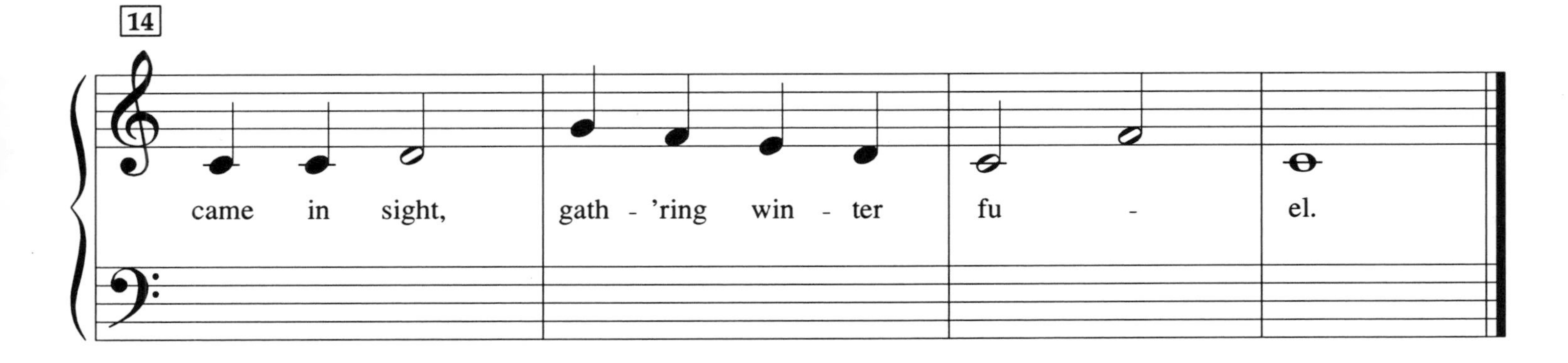
14
came in sight, gath - 'ring win - ter fu - el.

7
10

14

The Holly And The Ivy

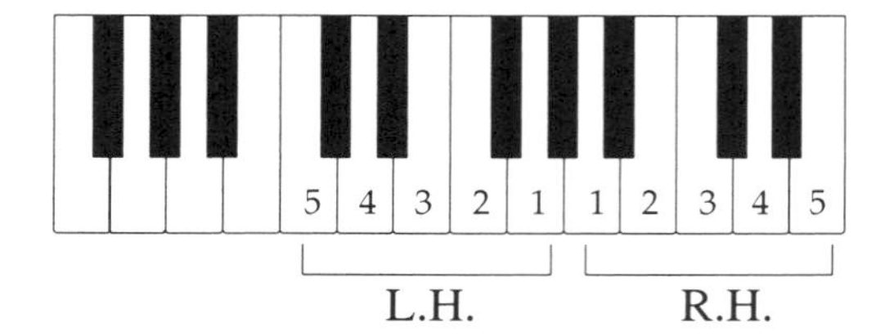

Traditional

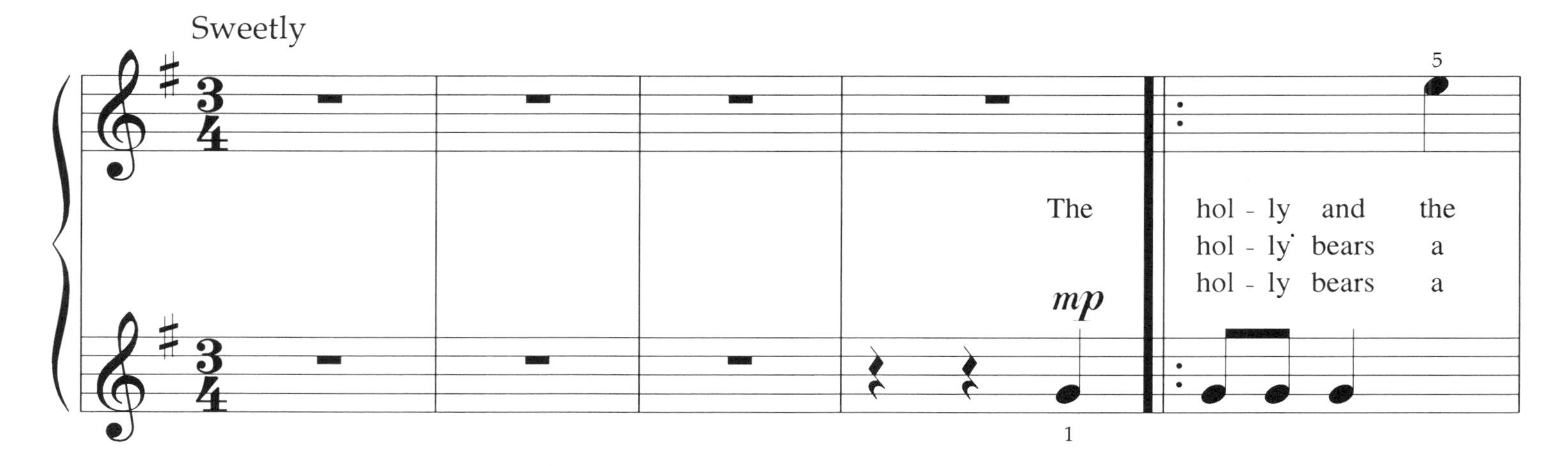

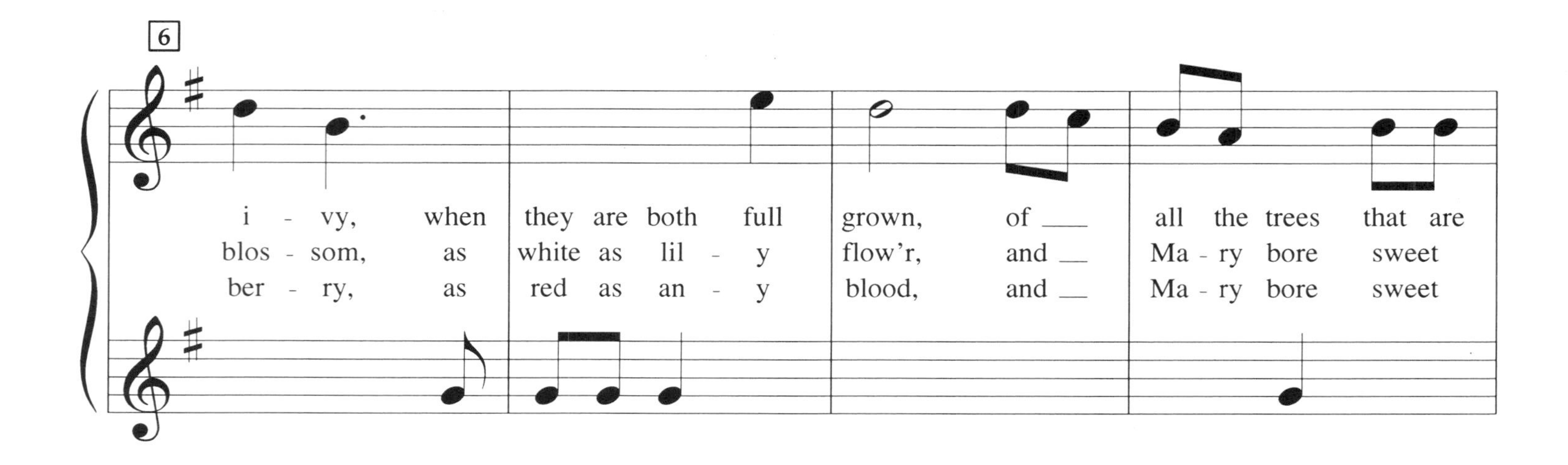

Duet Part (Student plays one octave higher.)

10
in the wood, the
Je - sus Christ, to
Je - sus Christ, to
hol - ly bears the
be our sweet Sav -
do poor sin - ners
crown.
iour.
good.
The
ris - ing of the
14
sun and the
run - ning of the
deer, the
play - ing of the
18
mer - ry or - gan, sweet
sing - ing of the
1.,2.
choir.
The
The
3.
choir.
10
14
18
1.,2.
3.

O Little Town Of Bethlehem

Words by Phillips Brooks
Music by Lewis H. Redner

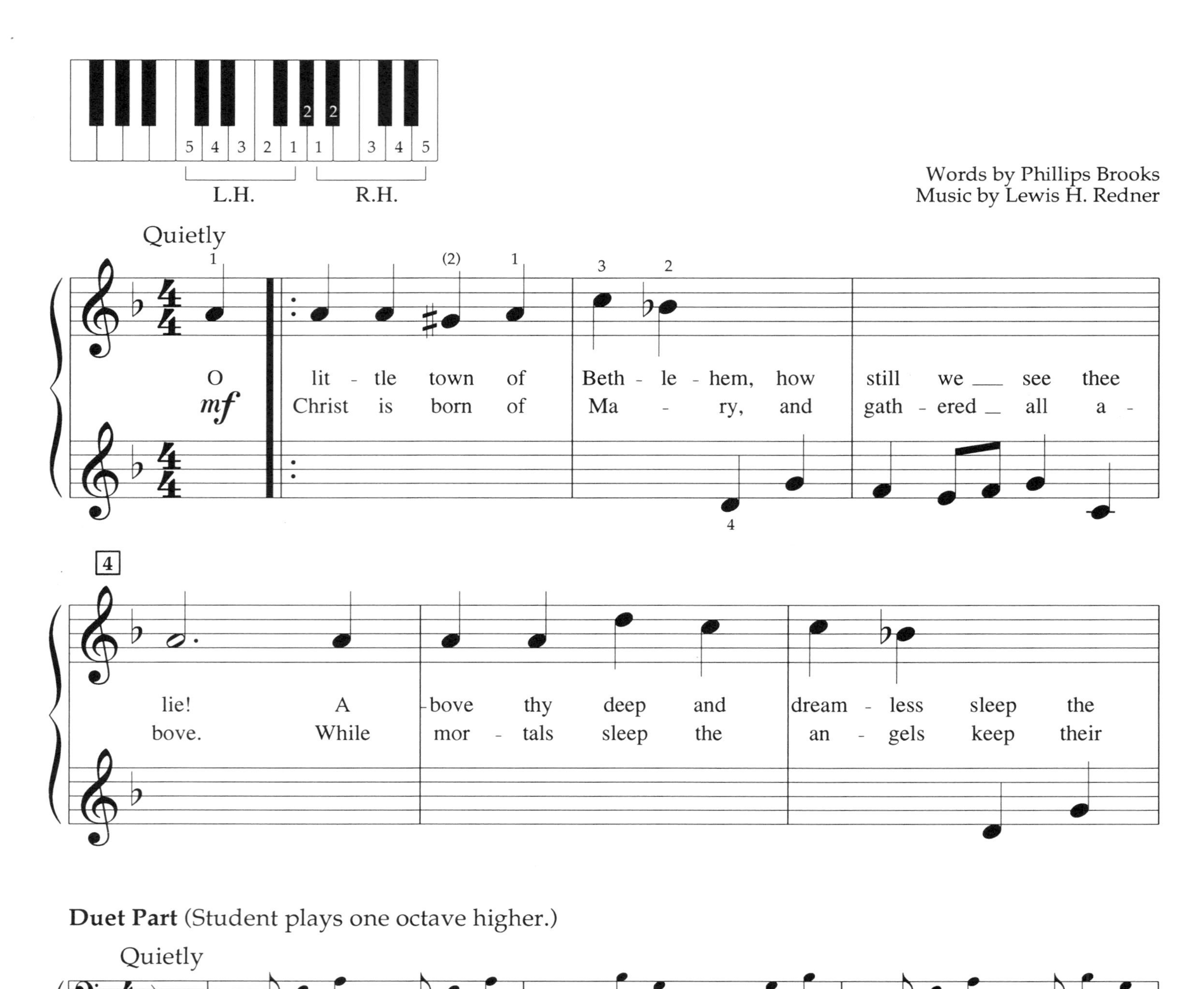

Duet Part (Student plays one octave higher.)

7
si - lent ___ stars go by. Yet in thy dark streets
watch of ___ won - d'ring love. O morn - ing stars, to -
10
(2) 1
shin - eth the ev - er - last - ing light. The hopes and fears of
geth - er pro - claim the ho - ly birth! And prais - es sing of
14
1.
2.
all the years are met in thee to - night. For
God the King, and peace to men on earth!
7
10
14
1.
2.

Still, Still, Still

Traditional Austrian Folk Tune

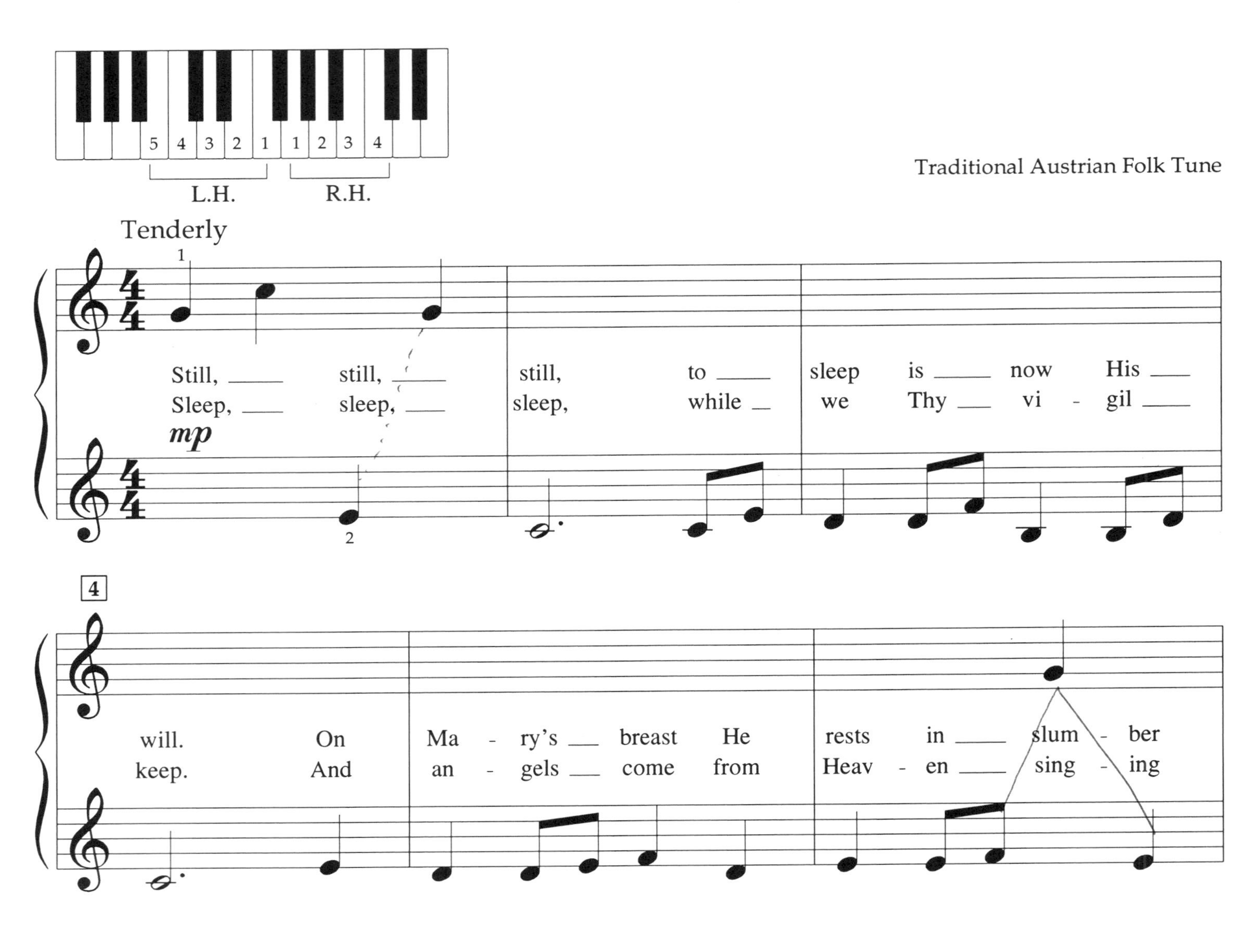

Duet Part (Student plays two octaves higher.)

7
while we pray in end - less num - ber. Still, still,
songs of ju - bi - la - tion bring - ing sleep, sleep,
10
1.
2.
still, to sleep is now His will.
sleep, while we Thy vi - gil keep.
14
Sleep, sleep, sleep, while we Thy vi - gil keep.
rit.
7
10
1.
2.
14
rit.

What Child Is This?

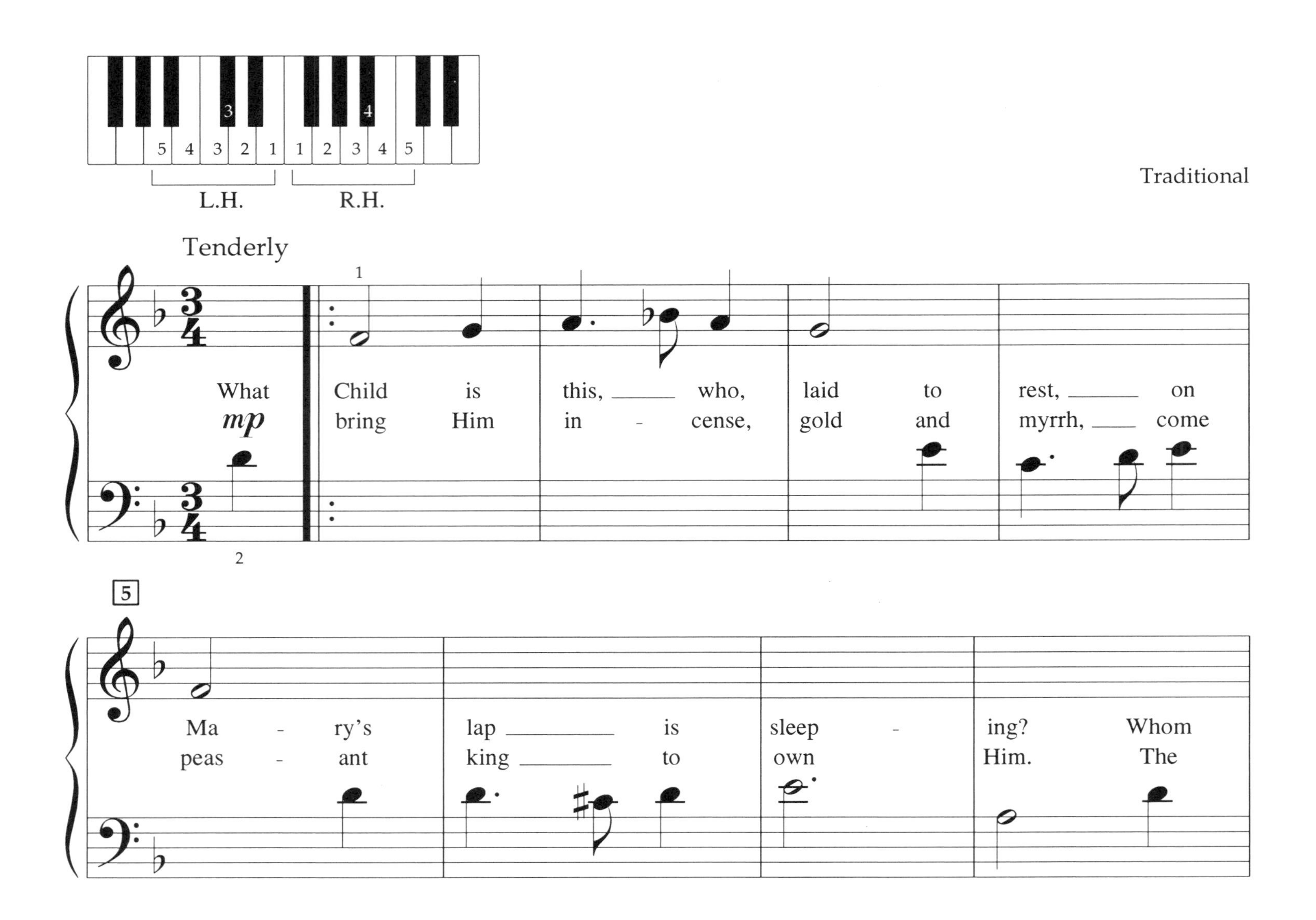

Duet Part (Student plays one octave higher.)

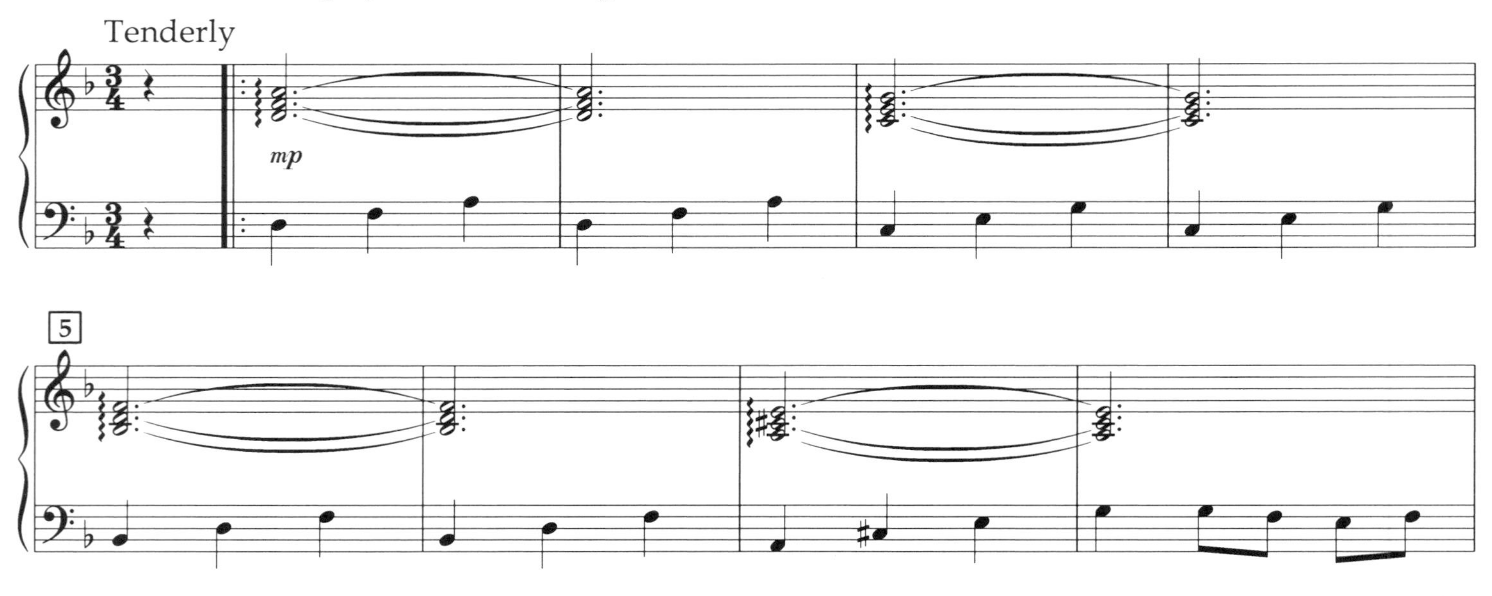

9
an - gels greet with an - thems sweet while
King of kings sal - va - tion brings, let

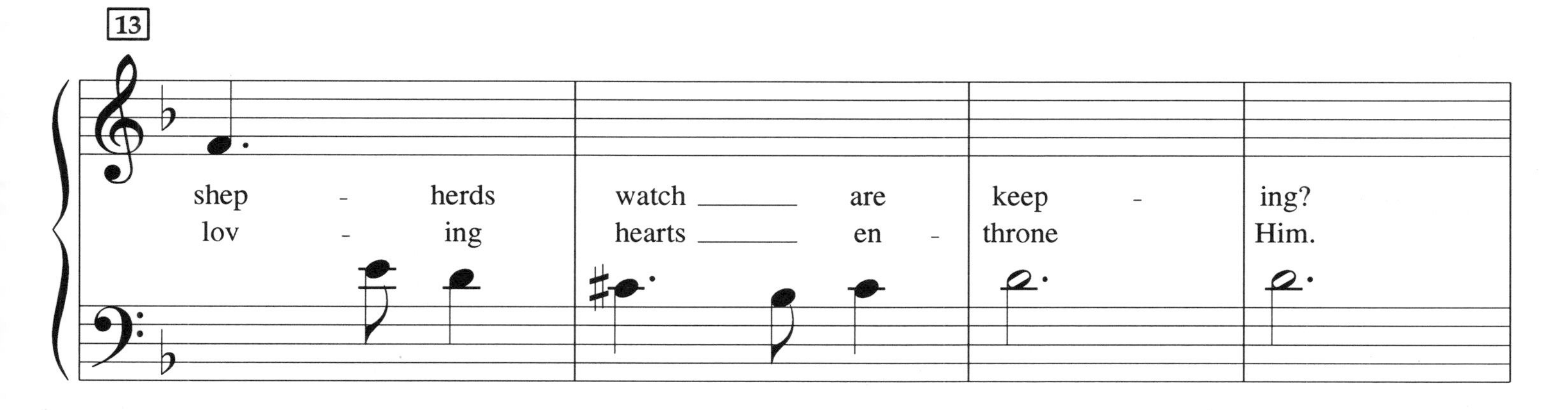
13
shep - herds watch are keep - ing?
lov - ing hearts en - throne Him.

17
This, this is Christ the King, whom
Raise, raise the song on high, the

9
13
17

21
shep - herds guard and an - gels sing.
Vir - gin sings her lul - la - by.
25
Haste, haste to bring him laud, the
Joy, joy for Christ is born, the
29
1.
2.
babe, the son of Ma - ry. So
babe, the son of Ma - ry.

21
25
29
1.
2.